Story in Literary Fiction
A Manual for Writers

by

William H. Coles

Bloomington, IN Milton Keynes, UK

AuthorHouse™
1663 Liberty Drive, Suite 200
Bloomington, IN 47403
www.authorhouse.com
Phone: 1-800-839-8640

AuthorHouse™ UK Ltd.
500 Avebury Boulevard
Central Milton Keynes, MK9 2BE
www.authorhouse.co.uk
Phone: 08001974150

© 2007 William H. Coles. All rights reserved.

No part of this book may be reproduced, stored in a retrieval system, or transmitted by any means without the written permission of the author.

First published by AuthorHouse 5/14/2007

ISBN: 978-1-4259-8664-3 (sc)

Library of Congress Control Number: 2007901334

Printed in the United States of America
Bloomington, Indiana

This book is printed on acid-free paper.

TABLE OF CONTENTS

Introduction   3
   A. The story in literary fiction   3
   B. The essence of a great storyteller   4
   C. Author's attitudes: fine-tuning   4

Part I Structuring the Story   9
   A. Know the story before writing   9
      1) Conflict   9
      2) Change and discovery   9
      3) Achieving goals   10
      4) Instilling creativity   10
      5) Realistic approach to writing   10
      6) Avoid elevated prose   10
   B. Outline   11
   C. Creating Scenes   12
      1) Conflict/action/resolution   13
      2) In-scene and narrative telling of conflicts   13
   D. Establishing time   14
   E. Setting   18
   F. Characterization   19
   G. Plot   26
      1) Basic plot structure: beginning, middle, end   26
      2) Transitions   29
      3) Drama   30
      4) Desire and motivation   31
      5) Inner (emotional) and outer (action) plots   31
   H. Dialogue   32

Part II Providing for the Reader   37
   A. How a story comes to life   37
      1) Learning about life   37

2) Reversal	38
3) Entertainment	38
4) Reader involvement	38
5) Action	39
6) Value	39
B. Story: Theme and Meaning	40
C. Narration of a story	43
D. Point of view	50
E. Engage the Reader	58
F. Distance	59
G. Voice	60
H. Space in the story for the reader	61
I. Sentimentality in writing	63
J. Drama in narration	64
K. Action	65
L. Language	67
1) Clichés	68
2) Word choice	68
3) Syntax	69
4) Spelling and grammar	69
5) Formatting	69
M. Process of revision	70
Appendix 1 Writing in the Moment	77
Appendix 2 Scene Examples: Variations of Narration, Point of View, Distance, Voice, Tense	81
Appendix 3 Sample Outlines	97
Index	99
Acknowledgement	105

Introduction

A. The story in literary fiction

Stories are told for many reasons—information, pride, teaching, rendering, warning, entertainment, intimidation. In its basic form, a story starts, something happens, and the story ends. But authors of literary fictional stories have more to consider. The literary fictional story builds on the evolution of the story from Greek poetic narratives, Biblical stories, Greek stage drama, medieval sung tales, folk tales, and the development of the written novel and short fiction from the eighteenth century to today.

Actually, written words are an awkward way to tell a story—and the telling is hard to do well. But the successful literary story gives the reader special benefits of enjoyment and memorability, and it provokes thought at levels no other form of storytelling does.

A literary story is neither a memoir that tells the truth of what happened nor genre fiction such as mystery, romance, detective, or science fiction that must restrict itself to precise reader expectations. Literary stories emerge from the author's imagination with strong characters who drive the plot and involve the reader. The literary story is an art form that should be preserved and allowed to evolve; it is created in the universe of imagination and provides maximum enjoyment and enlightenment for the reader. It stands alone.

This manual is dedicated to the creation of a great literary story that provides enjoyment and enlightenment for the literary reader and contributes to our literary heritage.

B. The essence of a great storyteller

Writers please readers by telling stories that are enjoyable and memorable. To be memorable, a story must have some emotional and intellectual impact. When a great story is finished, readers believe nothing in their lives will ever be exactly the way it was before they experienced the story. This awe-filled awareness comes from a new recognition or reversal of thinking, or a feeling that emerges when characters face conflict in the story that they resolve in meaningful ways.

The true significance in a story is in the quality of the telling, not by the elevated style of the prose.

For good storytelling, stories must be structured to provide continuous and total enjoyment to the reader through unified character action. The reader must be compelled to go on.

C. Author's attitudes: fine-tuning

To reach maximum potential, authors of fiction must discover who they are and why they write. In many ways, the telling of fictional stories is a performance that can be damaged or destroyed by ill-conceived attitudes about writing.

CORE QUESTIONS

Do I write to master the skills and concepts of writing as an art form (or do I write stories to explain experienced emotions)?

Great stories are dramatically constructed art forms—a sculpture in words—that produce enlightened change in characters and readers. Stories are not beautiful descriptions of abstractions lived—such as love, hate, revenge, jealousy. And stories are not created to purge the author of an emotional or intellectual crisis.

Do I strive to tell a creative fictional story based on imagination (or am I writing a memoir or biography)?

The memoir is a popular and legitimate form of writing. But writing a memoir requires skills that often conflict with imaginative fiction. Adherence to the truth of what happened or the belief that a story based on a true story is equal to, or superior to, the created fictional story, are destructive attitudes for the fiction writer. Most great stories are not just told from life; great stories are ideas (that may be stimulated by life) successfully expressed by creating dramatic (and significant) series of fictional events.

Do I write for creative excellence (or for fame)?

All authors want recognition for their work. But that recognition should be for writing stories that entertain and enlighten. Desire for fame as an author that comes from marketing and self-promotion imposes restrictions on creation of a great story. Writing a story is a selfless process and, above all, poor writing should not be promoted to the uninformed as worthy.

Do I write to provide meaning through entertainment and enlightenment (or to persuade to some presumption)?

To persuade a reader to a preset opinion does not support the creation of a great story. Authors enlighten about human nature; essayists, editorialists, and columnists persuade readers to opinions. Fiction authors who insert unrelated opinion in their stories face the danger of propaganda (deceptive or distorted information often about policy, ideas, doctrines or causes).

Do I rewrite to improve my creative story skills (or do I revise to transform my prose into obscure text with an intellectually intense meaning)?

Stories fail because of ineffective characterization or incredible conflicts and actions. Stories rarely fail because the prose is not fancy enough. Yet most authors revise through prose adjustment in style and craft when valuable revision really comes from structural adjustment, clarity of intent, and idea change.

Do I believe stories are dramatic events for a reader to experience (or written words for the reader to interpret)?

Fictional stories entertain and enlighten through drama—drama is conflict, action, and resolution. Readers become involved in the story; readers do not simply observe the story. The writer's challenge is to engage the reader from story beginning to end, not to describe events. Successful writers actually provide only enough information on the page to stimulate the story in the reader's mind. It is one of the wonders of reading great fictional stories that for each reader the story interpretation is unique to that reader and based on the reader's intelligence, experience, and creativity.

Do I believe stories are structures whose unity is discovered as reading progresses (or that they are meandering observations described step by step)?

Authors who start a character on a plot line to see what their characters will do have limited themselves for creating a story. Stories are carefully constructed and then present details that are chosen to create images and ideas in the minds of the reader. Details are not chosen just to record them. Stories can be thought of as jigsaw puzzles where the author supplies essential, clearly detailed pieces that are complete, accurate, interesting, and dramatic, and the reader fills in the rest.

Authors who insist that a nonstructured way is best for them—and then prefer to write rather than structure-and-write—miss the potential of reader enjoyment that is made possible by a well-constructed fictional story.

Proper attitude is essential: write a story as a unit, not as loosely associated ideas discovered moment by moment.

Part I

Structuring the Story

A. Know the story before writing

1) *Conflict*

An author is not simply presenting scenes and events by describing an imagined reality. Authors create stories by imagining characters and what they do in a story in a dramatic way. Historically, drama requires conflict, action, and resolution, and drama provides the essence of literary fiction. The conflict can be physical, mental, or emotional. The action is presented by placing the reader in the scene or by narrative telling, and resolution involves a change in the character, either a reversal of some thought or trait in the character or the character's recognition of something not understood before. It is in drama that the reader becomes involved and where, through the actions of the characters, readers sympathize with the characters.

2) *Change and discovery*

An effective story is a dramatic unit made of dramatic parts (scenes). It is in well-constructed scenes that characters with strong desires face significant conflicts. As the story progresses, the character's action and resolution of the conflicts bring a change in how the character thinks. In the best stories, the reader's thinking is changed (reversal) or he or she discovers something (recognition) by the logical progression of characters through scenes.

3) *Achieving goals*

A goal for the story is essential. When authors clearly know what they want to achieve with a story, writing is more targeted for the reader's understanding and readers enjoy the story more. The goal may change many times during the writing of a story. That is part of the healthy process of writing.

4) *Instilling creativity*

As previously noted, many authors reject structuring their stories before writing, arguing that discovering the story line as they progress is the best way to stimulate their creative process. But use of structure does not diminish creativity. In fact, thinking of the structure of the story before and during writing creates alternatives that can contribute significant, believable events to the story.

5) *Realistic approach to writing*

The challenge is to find the story, imagine it in images and scenes, and then write. Remember: great stories are not found by wandering through the writing process describing event after event as it comes to mind, and commenting on how characters feel.

6) *Avoid elevated prose*

Failure to structure is almost always replaced by ineffective elevation, that is inaccurate words exaggerated for meaning of the prose. Elevated prose downplays action and drama as the source of reader satisfaction and involvement.

In essence, in great stories, prose is not the endpoint.

B. Outline

An outline is a list of main-point story elements that organizes scenes, establishes timelines, tracks characters, superimposes emotional arcs in the story, embeds conflict, and includes whatever else may improve a story by logical, dramatic presentation. Outlines may be entirely a mental process, but a written outline is a valuable tool for authors. An outline helps authors to understand and to reflect on the story being told.

A story is a series of well-defined fragments. The quality of these fragments, for the reader, is improved if the fragment is developed within the context of the overall story, and not as an isolated story event or idea. Every element created affects every other element. As elements come together, theme and meaning emerge from the story. An outline helps achieve coherence in the writing.

Principles*-outline*

*Emotions, images, drama, time, and character-driven plot are all elements kept in mind when forming an outline.
*Stories are all elements working together as if they were not elements.
*Structure makes elements more effective.
*Elements in outline help identify the beginnings of meaning and theme.

Guidelines*-outline*

1) Test yourself: can you tell a summary of the story verbally without notes?
2) Do you know when a story will start and end, and all that happens in between, before you write?
3) What is the major conflict of the story (in a novel there may be many). What is the action precipitated by this conflict, what is the resolution of the conflict? Are you clear what the resolution is (even if you expect it to change as the story develops)?

C. Creating Scenes

Scenes are dramatic units that make up a story. As sentences are to paragraphs, scenes are to stories: they are the building blocks that contribute to the theme and action of the entire story.

1) Conflict/action/resolution

Conflict is the basis of a scene. Conflict is best developed between two or three (or more) characters; it is rare for a single-character scene to provide deep and intense conflict for the reader to become involved in. Conflicts can be physical, emotional, mental, or verbal.

Action presents how characters respond to conflict. How characters act in scenes reveals the characters' personalities so the reader develops respect and sympathy for characters.

Resolution of scene action tells the reader how the character was changed by the action.

2) In-scene and narrative telling of conflicts

In-scene development captures the reader's interest and provides maximum enjoyment. Yet in-scene development requires more time to read and more space on the page. Therefore narrative telling of scene conflict is useful in transitions and when time for in-scene development does not allow for smooth forward progress of the story. Most great stories have more in-scene development than narrative telling. (see Example 1)

Example 1: Narrative vs. In-scene

A) Narrative telling. (Quick, effective.)

> The ship sank.

B) In-scene showing. (More story time, more engaging.)

> The ocean liner listed, taking on water through the hole the torpedo made in her portside. The bridge shuddered from two explosions in the engine room, and as the crew struggled to release the lifeboats, the bow disappeared beneath the surface first, soon followed by the hull.

D. Establishing time

Every reader needs orientation in time as the measure of existence—birth to death for humans, from start to finish for anything. Stories describe what happened in the way humans experience time, but almost all stories are told in a shorter time than the story would take if lived; therefore, the stories are condensed (and parts are left out). Scenes, paragraphs, dialogue—all time-related elements—are altered from real-time progression.

Story time.

Story time is almost always chronological from start to finish. Readers must know when the story takes place—date, time.

Flashbacks (back story) happen before the start of the story. When flashbacks are multiple and/or extended, story time can be confused for the reader. Flashbacks should be used sparingly.

Character time.

Each character has a life lived, so that readers need to know characters' ages. Age gives clues about the characters' mental, emotional, and physical states—and since characters speak differently throughout their lives, age helps establish an effective, consistent, and realistic voice for each character.

In addition, each character uses chronologic story time that must be proportional to the character's importance in the story and in relation to other characters.

Narrator time.

Narrators relate stories from a certain time in their imagined lives. The narrator time, for best distancing and maximum effect, should be different than author time. The author creates in 2007 a story that is set in 1961. The narrator might tell the story as if telling is in 1972. The author does not need to state these relationships, but they should be well established in mind. Authors should at least think of these relationships for best dramatic effect and accurate characterization.

Reader time.
How long will the reader spend with the story and is it reasonable time spent for the story being told? A detailed epic rarely works in short fiction, and a second in a protagonist's lifetime can rarely be drawn out into a novel without losing reader interest.

Time logic.
All the aspects of time in a story must be logical in sequence so that cause and effect is believable. For barebones examples, a happening in 1994 cannot cause something to happen in 1993, or a character cannot fly an airplane that wasn't invented at the time of the story.

Author time.
Authors should allow sufficient time for story creation to make the story the best possible. Deadlines suppress great story creation.

Time condensation—narrative bridge
At times, detailed logical explanations will not fit into the storytelling. Narrative bridges can be used to avoid logical explanations. For example, you might have a character in a story who goes from point A to point B. Story time elapsed is six hours. The character might take a plane or go in an uninterrupted car trip at eighty miles per hour. But the character doesn't have her own car or enough money for a plane. Rather than work out the details of the character's solving the problem (assume it isn't important to the story) the reader will

often accept a brief narrative summary of the fact that character went from A to B. "Hester was determined to meet Harry in New York and she made the trip in six hours" might be used rather than showing her movement by plane or car and having to solve the credibility problems of how she paid for it.

Tense and time

All stories have happened. Even stories set in the future have happened in the author's mind. This is true also of present tense stories. Present tense is a useful device for telling a story that has already happened for a sense of immediacy.

There is a certain artificiality to present tense in a story, and readers will vary widely in their acceptance of stories told entirely in present tense. Present tense usage can also create an awkward orientation for the reader in time, including difficult transitions in and out of flashbacks. These time inconsistencies can also create doubt about the narrator's and character's perspectives and authority on story action.

In the moment

When writing in the moment, the reader is provided information filtered for the illusion of being in the time and place of the happening. This is not related to tense and either past or present can be used. In the moment relies on detail, adherence to minute description of the action in logical sequence, and time movement that approximates the pulse of real life.

For example: He struck the wooden match against the side of the matchbox in the dark, directed by habit. The glow from the flame illuminated the four-foot fuse. He placed the match to the fuse-end; the spark sputtered, and then the tight flame progressed with steady acceleration toward the bag that held the explosives.

E. Setting

Each story has a physical environment. How broad the choice for environment affects the way the story is told. A story in New York may require different development than a story in Peoria, because each setting is different and each has a different effect on characters and character action. Setting will influence the voice of the characters and the narrator.

Principles-setting

- *Carefully chosen settings allow opportunities for character and plot development—Mississippi in the 1960s carries the energies of racial strife, for example.
- *Excessive use of setting can detract from the momentum of a story and prohibit reader involvement.
- *Authors should be familiar with settings but should not choose romantic or exciting settings that do not contribute to the story. Never let travel-folder, awe-filled writing slip into the prose.

Guideline-setting

1) Settings are often emphasized by narrative description. Because narration is easier to write, for most authors, than other elements of fiction, there is a danger of too much setting detail with too many adjectives and similes. Be sure every detail of the setting does not just create an image of where the action is occurring but that it contributes to plot elements and augments character development.

F. Characterization

Characters populate stories and are developed through the accumulation of limited and carefully chosen facts and actions that interact with the reader's imagination to fill in gaps of characterization not directly provided. A delicate balance must be sought between information provided and information withheld. In order to provide enough information to allow the reader to know the character, enough room must be left open in the characterization for the reader to add their own imaginative details to complete their understanding of the character.

Every major character must have a serious desire (a strong want or need). These desires must be clear to the reader and related to the movement and theme of the story. When presenting character desires at a point in the story, to be effective the author must ask what the character knows at this point, and what the reader knows. The reader should always know more.

How characters come alive.

* Need for surprise.

In storytelling, authors need to structure a story so that every happening is a surprise for the reader, but the surprise must make the reader feel they anticipated the surprise all along (even though they didn't think about it). Readers cannot be manipulated. Readers must feel led, never forced, and led only to the point at which they can make their own discovery. All this is achieved by believable in-depth characterization, and by meticulous logic in the cause and effect of plot development. It is this difficult-to-achieve edge that makes the literary fictional story so special—and so difficult to write.

* Avoiding stereotypes for characters.

Readers subconsciously begin to group characters in knowable boxes based on the reader's life experiences—good or bad, likable or unlikable, smart or dumb, or moral or immoral. Unless the author provides sufficient characterization, readers will begin to pigeonhole characters, and the characters will become clichés. These stereotypical judgments are prevented, or adjusted, by the author's ability to create a unique, in-depth, acceptable character. When the author fails in character details, the reader's stereotyping works against the success of the story.

*Internal Reflection.

Internal reflection is a special attribute to the written story. The reader knows what a character thinks and feels. Internal reflection is a powerful storytelling technique if it supports the story. But it tends to be overused at the expense of character action, primarily because it is a way for the author—through the character—to say things important to him or her (the author) that are tangential or unrelated to story movement and theme.

How characters become credible.

*Acceptable responses.

As authors do their work well, a reader takes on a certain possession of the character. The character in any story starts out with unlimited options on things to do and say. But as the story progresses, these options narrow. The reader, enjoying the story, will not be aware of decreasing options, but they will be disturbed if the character does or says something that isn't what the reader would reasonably expect at that time in the story, and the reader's acceptance and caring for the character is diminished. If inappropriate character responses happen too often, the reader rejects the character and the story.

For example, Joe is a character who does

or says something in a story. Readers want to feel that they weren't exactly expecting Joe to do (or say) that, but now that he has, they can see exactly where he is coming from. Joe is "in character." His character.

The reader does not want to disbelieve Joe's character. When Joe is out of his character, the reader responds. He would never do (say) that. Not the Joe I know.

By the end of the story, the author has brought the reader to impact and character actions and dialogue will have few if any options. The character is so well formed, so deeply engrained in the reader, that the important late happenings—so crucial for meaning—must be reasonable for the character, even though the reader might not have anticipated them.

*Feelings.

Feeling, or emotion, is the prime tool of fiction. So expression of feelings is a key skill for the writer. The paradox is that erroneous expression of feelings can lead to sentimentality, and rejection of the story at the worst.

Feelings in a story can be told. "He was angry with her and told her so in a loud voice."

Although necessary at times, this telling of emotions tires the reader rapidly. It lacks energy. But the author can show feeling through action and dialogue, although this is so much more strenuous and time consuming for the author. For example, "You are the worst degenerate I've ever known." The dialogue here seems angry and hints that the anger is over a morality issue— interesting!

Feelings too must be toned to the character and the moment. Even slight inappropriateness will erode the reader's trust in the author to tell a good story.

For the most effective expression of feelings, abstractions such as love, anger, pity, hate, should be used with caution and the emotion expressed with concrete words and actions. For example, what do characters in love do? They have funny sensations under their sternums, they have more awareness of their heart-actions, their minds get clouded with details of the persons they love and they can't think about usual things. In essence, there is more impact to know love through actions--and words—than in naming the emotion. This is difficult to do because the descriptions of people in love are limited, and an author is always bordering on cliché. But the work to find the fresh descriptions right for the story is well worth the quality it provides for character development and plot vitality.

Every author must develop his or her own sensibilities about when feelings help the story. Character feelings are integrated with plot action in tasteful ways, and choices should be made that suit the reader who is best suited to enjoy the story. This is not just style-varnish; this is the essence of good writing.

Principles-*characterization*

*Characters are developed by action and reaction, dialogue, internal reflection, rhetorical question, emotions, diction (choice of words and context), narrative, exposition, integration with setting and description of scene, author's familiarity with the character's story line, back story, and other techniques unique to specific authors and particular stories.
*Desires must be internally powerful in order to force unavoidable action.
*Actions should convey character emotion for maximum effect.
*Throughout the story, characterization must be continuously layered on seamlessly and be true, interesting, and dynamic.
*Characters must be in conflict.
*One-character scenes are rarely, if ever, effective.
*As the character becomes stronger, that is more detailed and more familiar to the reader, the character's options for action and dialogue become less. Therefore, every author seeks good characterization for strong inevitable motivation of characters.

Guidelines-*characterization*

1) Be careful to show the character's desires, not to tell the desires, which is easier.
2) Be sure not to doom characters; they must have possibility to choose.

3) As characters move through a story, don't forget someone introduced earlier. Ask who hasn't been heard from for a while. Don't lose characters.
4) Although it is essential to use the point of view of a character for development, remember that too much access to one character's point of view can be deadening.
5) Remember that a character from life who is described with adherence to reality is limited in the dynamic, unique, fictional character development necessary in the best literary fiction.
6) Check character development by studying a unified overview all actions and dialog of the character in the story. Be sure that words and actions are driven by motivations that are right for the time in the character's development and are reasonable for the exact moment in the story. This is one of the most difficult skills to develop as a fiction writer, but it is the key to developing an identity as an author.
7) Be aware of inappropriate responses in dialog among multiple characters—especially of words, syntax, and ideation. Each character's response must fit the immediate range of emotions of all the characters at that story moment. When character responses are right, setting, other characters' feelings, reader enjoyment and acceptance, and even basic momentum of the story are enhanced.

G. Plot

In general, plot may be thought of as everything that happens in the story. But in literary fiction, characterization is the main element of plot; it is the inner story of characters that moves the outer story of plot action. Easy to say but difficult to do, mainly because to make the character's inner story believable, yet unique and forceful, takes skill and practice.

Common plot types in genre fiction (for example, search, revenge, rivalry, quest, mystery, and others) do not require development of characters to the same emotional level needed in literary stories. This helps make literary stories unique where characters' thoughts, emotions, and actions generate the plot. In genre plots with predetermined action the characters often act without regard to inner conflicts.

1) *Basic plot structure: beginning, middle, end*

a. Beginning

A beginning is that point in a story from which everything follows. Nonadherence to this major concept is a common misstep by an author. In essence, don't leap back in time to the past to start a story. Strive for unity that doesn't jerk the reader back and forth in time.

Principles - *beginning*

* The first sentence must be interesting.
* Always try to introduce major characters first, or early, in the work.
* Authors should begin with as much knowledge of where the story is going as possible; readers need a sense of story destination.
* Exceptions are published, but in general, stories should: (1) never start with a flashback, and (2) never start with the past perfect tense (he had plastered himself and his motorcycle against a brick wall) or (3) a negation (Billie could never climb the play gym as well as Suzie).
* Dialogue essential to the reader can provide effective characterization, but does not easily set the place, tone, and direction of a story. Avoid using dialogue to start a story.

b. Middle

This is the arc of the story, where it is essential to stay on the story track.

Guidelines-*middle*

1) Avoid temptations to wander when writing scenes and don't slip in ideas not important to the story.
2) Be sure character emotional and action progression is smooth and logical.

3) Keep looking for the theme.
4) Don't use extraneous detail.
5) Don't fall into excessive narrative description of your story.
6) Stay in the scene wherever possible to maintain drama and a sense of movement.

c. End

An ending is the point after which nothing else of significance happens in the story.

Principles-*ending*

*Endings must have elements of surprise yet must not be too surprising. An ending should be reasonable yet not too predictable. An ending should not be too devastating or too redemptive, but should have some recognizable—and memorable—change in one or more major characters.
*Stories must not fall apart at the end; an author should direct the reader's feelings. Readers should discover something new and unique to them. Therefore, for maximum impact, endings should show emotional and intellectual awakenings and reversals, not tell them.
*Resolutions must be clear in order to satisfy the reader, and they must be directly tied to the conflict and be a result of the action.

*Avoid trying to evoke emotion in a reader by telling a character's state of mind through clichés and sentimental images; the drama and action of the story should be used to provide the reader with a meaningful emotional response (see Example 2).

Example 2. Ineffective ending with clichés and sentimentality.

With a heavy heart, he sat on the carcass of his dead horse, the weight of the world light compared to his grief, a grief that would only grow with time. True friendships can never be replaced.

2) *Transitions*

The art of transition is essential to good storytelling. In film, the story goes from scene to scene and the visual orientation to time of day and place is immediate. In literary fiction, however, the reader must be oriented to each scene—who, what, when, where—by transitions. Transitions must tell the reader how much story time has transpired, and transitions must be logical, accurate, and factual.

Transitions lead the reader from one time to another, from place to place, and from emotion to emotion. Line spaces in formatting (and with markings for section or chapter breaks) are also used for transition, but these breaks should be careful chosen and not replace the well-written transition that is needed to enhance the story and the reader's understanding.

Guidelines-*transitions*

1) Tell the reader who or what is in the transition, when it occurs, and/or where it happens.
2) Do not try to create suspense by using personal pronouns—he, she, or they—without a clear and juxtaposed antecedent. Use "John drove..." rather than "He drove..." whenever it is appropriate.
3) Transitions usually condense action or description; be careful to include only the most important information in the transition. Transitions, by design, must be succinct.

3) Drama

Drama is conflict with a resultant reaction and an eventual resolution. Drama is the essence of a good story. Yet drama is more difficult for a writer of prose than for a dramatist or screenwriter, because the writer is restricted to the written word and cannot rely on visual and auditory stimuli. But overcoming the difficulties is rewarding for the writer because the intensity of the written word between author and reader can uniquely give powerful and memorable stories rarely achievable in film or stage drama.

Conflicts can be multiple or single, simple or complex; they may be person against any of the following: person, family, self, reality, friend, enemy, environment, values, morality, lust, authority, and others.

Action is best shown in-scene with occasional narrative summary for condensed action.

4) Desire and motivation

Characters must have strong desires (more than just needs) that motivate them to make significant changes. This strong desire must be explored as the story develops. With story development, careful narrowing (and concentrating) of the characters' desires strengthens the logic and acceptance of what happens in the story and to the character at every level.

Writers almost always discover that the first and second desires they discern for a character are weak clichés. This occurs because the desires are not thought out enough or targeted accurately. Only after digging deeply into the story, and only after layers of characterization have been created, can the perfect desire of a character be discovered.

5) Inner (emotional) and outer (action) plots

Principles-*plot*

Emotional (inner) story
* The plot line is dependent on good characterization. It represents the emotional flow of the characters. It generates and explains motives.
* All thoughts and emotions should be reasonable to the character's life, education, and intelligence. Errors will reduce the emotional impact and believability of the character.

Action (outer story)
* The outer story is dependent on conflict, action, and resolution. It should be logical and have evidence of clear cause and effect. Careful choice of in-scene or narrative telling is crucial for good storytelling.

H. Dialogue

Dialogue in fiction is not the way people speak in real life. Transcribed speech tends to be flat and boring. Dialogue in fiction must meet its responsibility to the storytelling, must be interesting, and must serve multiple purposes. These purposes include exposition (description of basic facts), time orientation, scene placement, sensory perceptions, emotional states, conflict, characterization (how a character speaks, thinks, or feels), plot advancement, theme support, enlightenment (of character and reader), and others that authors discover as they write that are specific to each new story (see Example 3 and Example 4).

Fiction dialogue must meet readers' expectations; dialogue must also be appropriate for the story style and individual characters' personalities, and the dialogue must seem real in their world.

Story in Literary Fiction

Example 3. Failed dialogue.

> "Is that a bear?" Joe asked.
> "Where?" Sam said.
> "Over there."
> "Damn. I think it is a bear."
> "What are we going to do?"
> "I don't know."

Example 4. Dialogue with elements of surprise and action.

> The bear reared back on its hind legs, roaring.
> "Don't move!" said Joe.
> "I'm going to throw up." Sam said.
> "He's seen us."
> "I dropped my rifle."
> "Start making noise. Maybe we can scare him."

The reading of the dialogue may take longer than the story action would require. The reader senses this discrepancy and although the discrepancy may not be identified, it may result in the feeling of inferior writing and storytelling.

But great dialogue can add a physical rhythm to the reading, provide a rich field for fictional voice development, show unique character thought patterns, and provide scene motion.

Characters speaking in fiction must say only what they can reasonably be expected to think and formulate. Thoughts, feelings, opinions, or desires of the author must not come through character dialogue.

Although you can easily find examples of authorial intrusion in many famous and published authors, it is rarely effective in present-day storytelling. Authorial intrusions weaken the character, break the reader's involvement in the story, and rarely contribute to the story line, theme, or development. This does not mean a narrator's prevailing presence is not always in the story, or that narrator's point of view is not useful. It is only jolting unrelated or tangential authorial ideas or speech inappropriate for the character and interjected into the flow of the story that must be avoided.

Principles-dialogue

* *Dialogue should never be written to fill in or to replace essential facts or transitions.
* Each dialogue segment should have multiple purposes.
* Dialogue should present essential information for the story.
* Dialogue should be spoken by the most effective character for the immediate part of the story.
* Modern dialogue is not effective as soliloquy, or sermon, or exposition of fact.
* Dialogue must be in a consistent voice.
* Dialogue is used to break up narrative passages, but dialogue as boredom prevention is not effective.

Guidelines-*dialogue*

1) To improve dialogue, ask what is the purpose. Does the dialogue advance the story? Does dialogue carry the action? Is an important tone established? Does dialogue orient the reader? Does dialogue contribute to characterization?
2) Dialogue must not sound like actors in a stage play. Actors have different rules. Their speech has different rhythms and is more restricted.
3) Dialogue must be constructed with attention to rhythmic effects that should be consistent with narrative and should contribute to the reader's process of reading the story. Excessive short dialogue between characters may give an unwanted and deadly rhythmic effect.
4) In effective dialogue, a character's question or idea should rarely be answered directly.
5) Modifiers used in attribution of dialogue should be tasteful. Avoid: "I love you," he humorously chortled.

Part II

Providing for the Reader

Principles

* The reader always wants a well-told, structured story with drama and freshness.
* Readers want clarity, logic, and believability; most readers of literary stories do not read to admire the author's facility with the language.

A. How a story comes to life

A story primarily tells a happening or a series of events, but a story is also a way of thinking, a structured means of communication. A story may embody one or more ideas to create a living environment for the reader.

1) Learning about life

Although it may be uncomfortable to think so, we are alone in our earthly existence—and for an alarmingly limited time. A human is born, eats, sleeps, and dies. Without ever being told why, we are locked alone inside our skulls during life. We are never given the privilege of thinking anyone else's thoughts, and being so isolated makes us intensely curious about what makes others tick. Stories give us a glimpse of how others think, and how others live their lives. As a result, we are guided in our own thinking and conduct.

2) *Reversal*

As each story forms, authors must think about what is in the story that will, in a classical sense, bring recognition or reversal of existing thought. A story loses life without significant reversal and becomes a hollow description of a happening that is too fatalistic and predictable. A good story leaves us with the sense that we know more than we did when we began reading, a sense of fulfillment brought about by involvement with others in a fictional environment.

3) *Entertainment*

Stories also entertain us. For all of us there are few things better than a good story well told. We read stories to discover memorable characters struggling for all the things we want in life—love, happiness, and longevity—and to see an exciting plot unfold; we crave to see how things will work out.

4) *Reader involvement*

Stories also succeed by involving the reader. A reader becomes a part of the story through emotional involvement with the characters and with the drama of the story, and the reading of the story becomes uniquely his or her own reading. This literary process is different than auditory and visual means of storytelling;

readers interpret the written words, translate meaning, and recreate their own story, one that is unique to their own experience and intelligence. Therefore, the writing must be clear and must be created with meticulous attention to provide the reader with as effortless a reading experience as possible.

Not every reader achieves this experience of immersion in a fictional story—with pleasure and reflection—that continues long after the story has ended. Many readers prefer the familiarity of recognizable story forms in which the detective solves the murder, a person loses love and regains love, or the monster threatens Gotham City and a flying hero saves the populace. In fact, some readers never devote the time or develop the experience to read literary stories capable of this intense meaningful reader involvement.

5) *Action*

Great storytelling is not just clever description of objects, people, and happenings. No adjective, no adverb, no alarmingly disjunctive position of words and phrases, will ever have more than a transient effect on the reader and will never create a memorable story. Great stories are about characters doing active things that change their lives. The action is not just what happens from scene to scene, it's what emotions inside a character (inner story) drive him or her to the unique actions on the page (outer story).

6) *Value*

A story must be worthy of the reader's involvement. The author must make the ideas, emotions, and action of the story inevitably force recognition or reversal in the character, and must make the story a significant stimulus to the reader's emotions so that the story will be remembered.

B. Story: Theme and Meaning

Definitions

> <u>Theme</u>—a distinct, recurring, and unifying quality or idea.
> <u>Meaning</u>—a psychological or moral sense, purpose, or significance.
> <u>Paradox</u>—a statement that may seem absurd but may be true, qualities that contradict, or something that conflicts with conventional opinion.
> <u>Morality</u>—standards of conduct that are accepted as right or proper.
> <u>Hero</u>—someone who acts with remarkable bravery, with great courage or with exceptional strength of character.

In structuring a great story, theme and meaning need to be thoroughly explored in order to clarify the presentation and to focus the epiphany (sudden revelation or insight). Character recognition of something new, and usually enlightening, and character reversal of thinking, intrigue the reader. Theme and meaning augment these effects.

In stories we have the need to create the unique situations of unexpected, above-average happenings in believable and acceptable ways. We need heroes. And all fiction requires characters to have at least a touch of the heroic (showing courage or determination) to move the action of the story to its conclusion. Comatose people don't make good characters. But all characters don't have to be hyperactive supermen either. No need to recreate Ulysses, Gandhi, or Abraham Lincoln. But the best characters can, and most often do, have a part of the hero in them, and that heroic part engages the reader and drives the story forward.

Heroism thrives when characters are put in difficult situations, and meaning is also enhanced in the heroic setting, because the actions of characters become more significant and often require strong morality. By thinking of heroic action, the author adds a dimension to the writing that creates the story.

Morality dominates every fiction story and the author's morality may be the same or different than that of the narrator's. The differences can provide the tension that results in stimulating prose. Character development, of course, is also related to the morality, or lack of morality, in the characters' lives.

Authors thinking about morality and how it affects their writing will both consciously and unconsciously insert meaning into their stories. Such meaning, as it is defined and becomes easier for the reader to grasp, is always beneficial to the writing as a work of art. If the author thinks about the story extensively, themes and meaning may begin to develop early. A unifying theme does not have to be identifiable by the reader; even a subliminal theme may have a powerful effect.

But caution is needed. Theme and meaning cannot be delivered with a heavy hand. As an example, moving characters through a story plot in order to express the author's opinion results in propaganda, and propaganda is not compatible with good fiction. In essence, literary readers do not want to feel the author's purpose is to persuade, even if they agree with the persuasion; readers want to be entertained and to enjoy themselves.

Guidelines*-theme and meaning*

1) Think through characters' actions and conflicts in the story to see if there are recurrent ideas and motivations that logically contribute to the theme.
2) Ask whether the moral overlay of your writing is consistent for the story you are creating.
3) Ask whether a moral theme becomes so apparent as to offend the reader. Readers back away from writing when they feel they are being asked to convert to a particular morality. The necessary morality of a story should stay well within the limits of what the characters and actions in the story would reasonably suggest.
4) Don't use your fictional story for overt moral or political purposes. The memorable enjoyable art form that is the literary story does not sprout from roots of moral or political purpose. Instead, it grows from significant and rewarding

insights into the human condition that makes the reader a better and more complete person.

5) Paradox (contradiction) can express both sides of an issue and is useful in fiction, but to use it with good effect, you must place it within a detailed and balanced presentation that is combined with dramatic writing.

C. Narration of a story

Authors create stories. Narrators tell the stories, either speaking (1) directly to the reader, or (2) through a character. Characters act in stories—they make plots develop—and they are used often to deliver story information to the reader.

Narration must orient the reader so that the reader is never confused and is always comfortably engaged in the story and thus able to develop a sympathetic connection to one or more characters. Reader sympathy with characters is a major source of reader tension. Readers want to know what will happen to someone they care about.

A narrator differs from an author in storytelling. This separation (author from narrator) is essential for good storytelling, enhances story authenticity, and helps provide tension.

There are many useful differences between author and narrator.

1) The date and time the narrator tells the story is often different than the date and time the author

creates the story. This affects the voices of characters, the quality and type of emotions revealed by the characters, the logic of character development and plot action, and the tone, opinions, and morality of the story.

2) The life of the author is different than the imagined life of the narrator. After all, authors telling their life stories are writing memoirs. Memoir writing in a literary story—even partially—detracts from the potential of the story. Both characterization and action can be more fully developed if there is no reliance on what really happened in the author's experience.

3) The author should not be the foil for characters' interpretations and opinions. A defined narrator will be more objective in story presentation, and the story's conflicts and themes can be more clearly presented through the techniques of fiction—in-scene action, dialogue, narration, and internal reflection.

Also, authors, like God in life, are omniscient in the story world. Such power is too heavy-handed for contrasting with a character. The character becomes diminished, often to the point of seeming ridiculous. Author separation from a story becomes essential when the author particularly feels strongly about a specific idea such as the existence of God, or the superiority of one gender.

4) The narrator has a distinct voice even if it is never directly presented to the reader. This voice is not the author's voice and it is not any of the characters' voices. The narrator speaks to provide critical story information to the reader that characters cannot know, and provides insight that a character cannot reasonably generate.

The presence of a narrator's voice is always beneficial to the story. (Example 5 and Example 6). Many authors will not think about how they narrate their stories, and the writing thus does not provide the reader with the clarity, impact, or enjoyment that it could provide.

Many authors ineffectively think there is no value in thinking of separate narrator and character when a story is written in the "first person" using an "I" character. But there are significant problems for authors writing in the "first person" that make this separation useful. First, distance.

An "I" character (first person point of view) can only provide information that is reasonably within the range of that person's senses of sight, hearing, taste, touch or feel. Ideas and information outside the senses must be imagined with conjecture.

When using the first person, whether deliberate or not, story truths can be conveyed to the reader in two ways. The author can use the first person as the sole provider of this information, which may require awkward constructions, or can simply supply the information in a narrator's voice and view.

There is narrator information in every first person story. Authors must be aware of how and when the information is delivered to create their best stories. But the reader should not be aware.

The second problem for first person characters is reliability. There are story-truths and there is a character's perception of story-truths. The reader of first person stories must judge the reliability of the first person character telling story truth.

First person characters strain credibility when they provide information that is, or may be, out of the range of their senses or experience.

As a general rule, narrators must be more reliable than characters, or the story loses credibility. So in the first person story, as in all stories, the author may provide information through the narrator. This helps the reader judge the character reliability in perceiving the story world. The most competent of authors understands this concept and uses it for characterization, tension, and meaning.

The third problem for first person characters is limitation. Some story worlds are too broad to be conveyed to the reader through the first person character alone. One person's view of the world is more restricted than two or more's views. When writing in the first person, most effective setting and other story details may be best provided when the author uses narrator supplied information.

Authors who write with a narrative concept in the first person strengthen the story by minimizing distance problems, having control of reliability issues, and by providing less restricted ideas. To be successful, the narrator aspect of the "I" character must be introduced early, always be present, and be consistently presented throughout the story. And it should be seamless, not as a trick of the author but as a gift to the reader.

Writers who insist that the collapse of narrator into the first person character—to act as a unit— is not only practical but essential, lose a control of their writing that is necessary for excellence.

5) If a narrator speaks directly to a reader, the purpose is to enhance the reader's understanding of the story. When authors speak directly to the reader there is danger of extraneous information and the reader will not see the information as supportive of the story. Narrators (created in the mind of the author) choose facts objectively that support the story and seek exactly the right word, the best turn of phrase, as well as absolute clarity and logic to provide drama and the tension. Narrators act as a filter for author intrusion.

6) The time of telling the story is often different for the narrator and for the author, just as it is for the narrator and the characters. The narrator's attitudes, sensibilities, social development, and morality will be specific to the time the narrator is imagined to be telling the story. The reader should always, at least, have an awareness of the time from which the narrator speaks in relation to story time.

Example 5. Narration. In-scene narrator.

> I told Phyllis to stand in the bathtub and hide behind the shower curtain as I locked the bathroom door from the inside—pushing a dime-sized cylinder that stuck out half an inch from the center of the handle. Outside the front door, the attacker clutched a tire iron in both hands. His first blow splintered the door panel. Phyllis screamed and grabbed my arm.

Comment.
This scene, exaggerated and a little awkward to make a point, is told through the "I" character. Many would argue this is "first person point of view." But there is a shift for the reader from bathroom to outside the front door back to the bathroom. The narrator, not the "I" character, is giving necessary information about what is happening outside the apartment. Of course, the confrontation could be filtered through the character's consciousness to avoid the narrator's contribution. For example, "I heard the door panel splinter and imagined the attacker clutching a tire iron." This construction is awkward.

Authors need to be aware of the difficult and complex relationship of narrator to first person and that narrators are not characters when constructing the effective story.

Example 6. Narration. From Charlotte Bronte's *Jane Eyre*, Chapter 11.

"A new chapter in a novel is something like a new scene in a play; and when I draw up the curtain this time, reader, you must fancy you see a room in the George Inn at Milcote, with a large figured papering on the walls as inn rooms have; such a carpet, such furniture, such ornaments on the mantelpiece; such prints; including a portrait of George the Third, and another of the Prince of Wales, and a representation of the death of Wolfe. All this is visible to you by the light of an oil lamp hanging from the ceiling, and by that excellent fire, near which I sit in my cloak and bonnet;" . . .

Comment.

Information provided using the "I" character as narrator. Note (1) the character could be used so the information is not necessarily the narrator's, and (2) the direct address of the reader, which is a technique now archaic.

Principle-narration

*Narration is the telling of the story and not a venue for admirable prose.
* In a memoir (or a partial memoir or creative nonfiction), authors describe personal events. They cannot alter events, and the injection of imagined events to augment drama and meaning are not possible. As a result, story intensity is often dependent on word description of the action rather than adjustments in the action that are available to the fiction writer.
* In fiction, authors create stories in the mind of the reader through a narrator telling the story with techniques chosen to provide the most reader enjoyment. Intensity is mainly dependent on imagined conflict and action.

D. Point of view

Definitions of point of view

1) A particular *position* in space, time, or development from which something is considered or evaluated
2) A particular manner of considering or *evaluating* something
3) A particular reasoned mental attitude or *opinion* about something

The term "point of view" in writing is usually used in a positional sense. First-person point of view means the "I" gives story information to the reader. Third-person uses a "he" or "she" pronoun. Narrators also give story information directly to the reader. But the "manner of considering" and "reasoned opinion" aspects are also always implied in writing from a point of view, and thus can be confusing. These aspects may not be within the character purview, and can confuse the reader as to who is really telling the story and how honestly it is being told.

Often the analogy of a camera position is used for point of view. A character (or sometimes a narrator) is thought of as a camera lens through which the reader is told the story. But when a character gives story information to the reader, it is often not exclusively in the role of a camera. The character selects details within that character's voice, intellect, and experience, and the character also tells unique thoughts and feelings

—neither is something a camera is capable of. Authors must consider these complexities in order to get the most out of storytelling and to avoid restrictive rules about point of view that deaden the vitality of the story.

It is natural, at this point in the discussion, to stubbornly rely on traditional academic teaching: that is, there are three points of view related to character—first person, third person, and omniscient; therefore, establish your point of view, stick to it, and develop characters and advance plot. Authors writing with this attitude will focus intently on revision for failures to adhere strictly to a point of view and miss the importance of other aspects of story telling. To remain rigid about point of view destructively avoids the strenuous thought needed for total comprehension of narration and the freedom it gives to the writer.

Point of view is a part of narration along with issues of distance (as it relates to a characters comprehension of action through the senses), voice, character reliability as a narrative tool in story telling, and solid development of theme. To embrace point of view alone without considering a narrator—is like a violinist playing a violin with one string—you may hear the melody but the overall effect falls short.

As point of view is established for the reader, so also is the reliability of the character tested—and accepted or rejected by the reader. The reliability of the character's perception of the story world is restricted to the five senses of the character—sight, touch, smell, taste, hearing--and internal thoughts and feelings. Inevitably information may be included in a story that is not clearly established as possible from a certain character's point of view. At times, an unreliable character telling an impossible story detail can create irritation in the reader and detract from the story. It is possible, however, for authors in full control of their writing to use lack of reliability as a character trait in ways that contribute effectively to story meaning and outcome.

Narrators, unlike characters, generally have to be reliable in storytelling. When the narrator is unreliable, the reader may feel manipulated or tricked. An unreliable narrator can emerge when the "I" character is the voice giving story details. Such a narrator may provide for interesting drama and story tension by leading the reader to beliefs and attitudes different between the characters and narrator, but only an author who is aware of the dangers of distracting and irritating the reader can develop unreliable narrators that benefit the story and the reader's experience.

The issue of character reliability also contributes to reader engagement in the story. As characters become increasingly questionable as to reliability, the reader's sympathy is less engaged. Readers' concerns about dangers to characters they sympathize with is the basic element for tension and drama in the story. These concerns make the reader care about the conflict and worry about the resultant action and resolution.

So the importance of narrator techniques—of point of view and the effect of distance and reliability—eventually dictate the degree of reader sympathy and the reader involvement in the outcome of the story's conflict.

As an author, thorough control of narration is essential for story success.

Story in Literary Fiction

Principles-*point of view*

* Point of view is a tool and should not be restrictive. To insist on an unvarying, unitary point of view in telling a story risks: (1) amateurish writing, (2) demeaning good readers as unknowledgeable. Point of view categories are best thought of as one of the ways to orient the reader in the broader context of narrative forces moving the story forward.
* Point of view should be used creatively to give the reader story information directly and succinctly.
* The "omniscient" point of view (multiple points of view at various distances—close or distant—from the action) can be used without calling attention to itself as a technique and can provide maximum information to the reader (see Example 7 and Example 8).

Example 7. Multiple characters (often inaccurately referred to as omniscient point of view).

> The ball landed six inches inside the back line. From the crisp center-string feel when the ball left the racquet, he knew the ball was in even if he had his eyes closed.
> "Out," she called, looking to see if he would argue.
> "Nice call," he said, seething.

Comment.
"The ball landed six inches inside the back line." This is the narrator or a third person some distance from the action. "From the crisp center-string feel when the ball left the racquet, he knew the ball was in even if he had his eyes closed." This is the man through a limited close third person. (Distant third person might be: She saw the racquet vibrate in his hand when the ball hit center and he nodded satisfaction of a shot well placed.). "'Out,' she called, looking to see if he would argue." This is the woman through a close limited third person point of view. "Nice call," he said, seething. The man's point of view again. (see Example 8)

Example 8. Different points of view using the event in Example 7.

The entire event could be written in the woman's limited third-person point of view:

> The ball bounced inside the back line but she called "out," watching to see if he would argue.
> "Nice call," he said. Was he being a smart ass?

...Or entirely in limited third-person male character point of view:

When the ball left his racquet with a perfect trajectory, he knew it was in but she called it out, staring at him intently. What did she expect?

"Nice call," he said sarcastically.

...Or entirely in first-person point of view:

I sat on a chair near the sidelines drinking Gatorade. Rob hit the ball. It landed six inches inside the baseline. He would know without even looking that the ball was in. "Out," Alice called as Rob flushed. "Nice call," he said and he hit a drop shot on the next point. I waited to see if she could figure out a way to cheat when it was so obviously in.

Principles–*"I" (first person) point of view*

* In first person, always ask how well the character knows himself or herself. Does she or he project self-knowledge well? The reader will be uncomfortable with a first-person narrator with deficiencies in narrative capabilities.
* In first person, do not let the story slip from narrator time to character time and back again. It is effective to create the story with different times for the narrator and the characters, and this is usually adult to child. When differences in time

of narration and character time are employed, readers almost always want the adult point of view to dominate.

*In first-person or third-person close narration, it is almost impossible to technically limit the point of view only to what the character can experience and think in the story. Many stories achieve this with a specific intent for sympathy in the reader. Other stories may achieve a limited (close, reliable) point of view but lose the opportunity to develop necessary detail outside. Try for what is best for your story, and don't adhere to a preconceived point of view that is detrimental to creating the best story possible. Think of our lives. We see only in front of us. We never see the back of us, the top, or the bottom, which others can see. We use tricks like mirrors and videos to see ourselves in ways that are physically impossible, and we use varying points of view to provide the reader with the best story information.

*When our thinking is limited in any way we fail to use our intelligence and our experience in life. To create stories with limitations such as strict point of view rules about writing is impractical and rarely effective. We live in the first person, but when we experience stories we frequently want more than a reasonable first person can give. In stories, readers often want to see beyond the limitations of one person's consciousness, because tension, through drama, is created partially by differences in perceptions.

Guidelines-*point of view*

1) If you transit from one point of view to another, is the transition firm but graceful? It is difficult to do well.
2) Is your point of view lifelike? If not, have you made the right choices regarding points of view in the story?
3) Don't use a reflexive point of view. Avoid these types of constructions: Mary saw he didn't know Marcie was sarcastic. Better: He flinched at Marcie's sarcastic words. If you are in a point of view, just state what happens. Avoid reflexive constructions: he noticed, saw, knew, wondered, thought, decided, and so forth.
4) Remember that point of view is not a box that the author must cram the story into. Point of view is a way of experiencing the story, and authors use whatever works for them to create the best story possible.
5) For tension in the story, are the differences between the narrator's point of view and the character's point of view clear to the reader?

William H. Coles

E. Engage the Reader

Many readers never achieve the experience of immersion in a fictional story. Many stories don't provide the clarity of telling or the inherent drama needed for the reader to be immersed. In fact, in the minds of many, the literary story contains excessive internal reflection—abstract, metaphoric, lyrical, static—that readers must work to follow. But the great literary story is vibrant with action, brimming with interesting characters, and can't be put down. The literary story engages the reader, not just to solve an unknown or see how a known plot ending will work out, but with concern for the resolution and character change, as if the characters were real and worthy of sympathy. This reader immersion has been called the continuous fictional dream. Not a bad metaphor, like going below the surface of a fluid fiction environment—specific to each story but similar in its effect on a reader—where characters come to life and do their thing with the reader right there with them.

The author must keep readers in the story and prevent breaking their unwavering involvement while reading. A reader loses total concentration when something throws them out of the story—like breaking the tissue or fabric of the story. Although these disruptive missteps can occur easily, and are sometimes unavoidable (authors can't please every personality), common problems can be prevented: missteps in characterization; illogical cause and effect; inaccurate, nonsupportive metaphors; wrong word choice; excessive narration when in-scene action is needed; authorial intrusion; obscure images; awkward syntax; and anything that causes the reader to pull back and wonder if that was right or whether that couldn't be better.

F. Distance

The narrator is narrating the story. The story is not the world. Yet a story has a defined space and the position of the reader in the story varies depending on the reader's relationship to the action. A reader can be given information close to the action, or far away.

Distance from the scene action can come into play when: (1) a narrator informs the reader of a distant or close perspective directly, (2) a character who orients the reader to distance from action is used by the narrator to present story information. The reader's distance from the action is created through word choice (particularly verbs and adverbs), type of images, character senses employed, and use of internal reflection. To erase reader discomfort caused by shifts in the distance from the action requires attention to transitions and the restructuring of scenes (see Example 9)

Example 9. Shifting distance (reader orientation) in a scene.

> George Wheeler was close to the center of the line of Yankee soldiers that charged the hill at Manassas. George on foot barely came to the knee of the lieutenant on horseback who

urged him into the line of fire. Ahead puffs of smoke drifted up into the air from the guns of the enemy George could not see. He fired his rifle without aiming at a clump of bushes and felt the hot metal of the gun in his hands. The heat of metal was different than the heat of Bobby's skin when he died, flushed with the fever from an infected belly wound. He pondered Bobby's death for an instant, distracted from the ever-increasing closeness of the enemy. The lieutenant spurred his horse forward so he was more exposed than any of the other line officers. The lieutenant's head jerked back; George knew the lieutenant was hit, knew the lieutenant was dead, and knew they were leaderless for the moment. He turned and ran.

G. Voice

Voice is everything a character, or a narrator, says, thinks, or feels in a story. Once voice is established for a character, only certain words and phrasings will augment a specific character's voice.

Lines from five different characters.

1) "There is nothing you could ever say that would deter me."
2) "I'm cool."
3) "Liar. No one will believe you."

4) "May God forgive your transgressions. Praise God."

5) "Make my day."

Each of the preceding lines has a different voice. Any one of these examples says something about the character. One line spoken by a character in a story must easily fit into all that has been thought and said by that character, and readers require consistency in this regard throughout the story.

Principle-voice

*Each character's voice, and the narrator's, must be consistent throughout the story. Pay attention to the character or narrator's word choice, syntax, slang, ideation, opinion, and the length and complexity of sentences and phrases.

H. Space in the story for the reader

The narrator must present the story clearly and succinctly to the reader so that the reader becomes involved—that is, so that the reader is pulled into the story. Space is made in the story for the reader to feel and care. A good story provides opportunities for the reader to use his or her imagination in the reading and interpretation of the story. These opportunities in the story are when the reader relates to character conflicts and begins to anticipate (and want) outcomes.

Principles-*space for reader*

*The narrator cannot withhold information. No carrots dangled before the reader to try to raise false tension. (Avoid: The automatic lay under her panties in her top dresser drawer, and Jim wondered why it was there. Was she capable of doing harm to another human being? Or even herself?)

*The narrator cannot be poetically excessive and vague. The narrator must use drama, meaning, conflict, action, and resolution to tell the story. (Avoid: As the attacker shoved the barrel end of the automatic into his mouth and released the safety, a cornucopia of fear tumbled through his brain.) Reaching for impressive (often Latinate) words or extraordinary metaphors that detract rather than augment the understanding—or using images unrelated to the story—makes for ineffective storytelling.

Guidelines-*space for reader*

1) Dissect the techniques of authors you admire who bring you into their stories.
2) Use the story narrator's perspective that is most effective for the best story. Here is where thoughts about distance, point of view, and voice are important to allow enough reader space.

I. Sentimentality in writing

Sentimentality (broadly—the tendency of indulging in emotion or nostalgia) is not an easy concept. For the author, sentimentality is emotions demanded of the reader that are not created through the interaction of believable characters in dramatic scenes. Sentimental writing uses stock images for emotion and clichés for descriptions of character emotions rather than the unique involvement of characters that makes the reader understand and share the characters' emotions.

Two realities work against the exclusion of sentimentality from fiction. First, many readers seek sentimentality (some readers are perfectly happy with images of babies with big sorrowful eyes and dogs with wagging tails). But the reader seeking higher levels of enjoyment that can only be achieved by a story created as an art form will not accept the manipulation of feeling that sentimentality evokes. Second, certain genres of fiction use sentimentality as a technique almost exclusively. For example, romance genre fiction is built on sentimental clichés and is enjoyable to many. But genre fiction is not a part of this discussion. In essence, for great art, the author must be able to create true emotional responses. (see Example 10)

Unfortunately, perceiving sentimentality is subjective; there are no totally dependable rules. Understanding sentimentality in one's writing comes from experience in reading and writing, and from developing a better understanding of valid situations and characters that provoke emotions.

Example 10. Emotions demanded and emotions implied.

Demanded sentimentality. Narrative.

> The sight of the scruffy woman's sores as she held out her hand for money made Marcie want to cry.

Implied sentiment. In-scene drama.

> The beggar sat cross-legged reaching up with an open shaking hand. The sores on her palm were wet and contagious. Marcie stepped back and took a dollar bill from her purse, dropping it toward the hand from a safe distance. The bill settled to the ground five feet from the beggar, who lunged forward, her body covering her reward.
> Marcie dug into her purse again and handed a ten dollar bill to the beggar before she walked away.

J. Drama in narration

Drama is conflict, action, and resolution.

Principles-*drama*

*In modern fiction it is generally not useful or acceptable for the author to speak directly to the

reader. It disrupts the dramatic flow of the story.
*The narrator controls the storytelling, and scenes must relate to one another so that tension will transfer through the story. The arc of the story must remain intact.
* Discrepancies between character, reader, and narrator thoughts create tension (about the story and about life).
*Tension can be created by differences in the reliability of the narrator and the characters. The narrator should be the more reliable one.

K. Action

Stories must have action. The author uses dramatic structure to keep the story moving with conflict, action, and resolution, and the author keeps the reader in a defined story-present by minimizing recall and reflective discovery of past conflicts.

Guidelines-action

1) Stories in the main should be told in-scene and not in narrative description. (see Example 11). Readers are engaged by in-scene writing. But they are often denied the pleasure of being included in the writing because (a) using narrative writing is easier and the reader is quickly bored, and (b) narrative writing lends itself to complicated, over-extended prose that the author often

enjoys writing but that irritates the reader ("She crashed the party like a freight train without brakes" is almost always not as effective for a story as "She entered the party through the back door of the apartment uninvited.").

Example 11: Narrative description versus in-scene writing. Compare these examples (with exaggerated prose to make a point) that illustrate the differences.

Narrative description (telling):

> Paul was jealous that Helen could sing with so much passion that others couldn't take their eyes away from her as she performed.

In scene (showing):

> Helen held the floor-stand microphone with both hands. The piano player played the introduction hunched over the keyboard. Helen took a deep breath and sang with a soft breathy voice, her eyes closed until the refrain when her gaze swept the audience of strangers, all watching her.
> She sang three verses and smiled at the end without a bow. The crowd applauded. Paul approached Helen as she climbed down off the stage.
> "I wish I could sing like that," Paul said. "I don't have your ear for perfection."

L. Language

Many authors of stories have not yet attained control of the language. Too often the author of creative fiction assumes a level of competence with the language that is not sufficient to create a unique, lasting, worthwhile work of art—the literary fictional story.

Good writing requires:

1. Exhaustive vocabulary.
2. Egoless self-criticism.
3. Perfect grammar. Grammar in English is not just a set of irritating rules; it is the structure by which we write effective English. If grammar is to be rejected as important in an author's writing, it can only successfully be from a position of total understanding. You must know the rule to break it. You can't say you don't need it because you're great without it. Readers know instinctively what you're up to.
4. A rhythmic sense.
5. Logical punctuation.
6. Resistance to writing like someone successful whom the author likes. (This is particularly true in revision. Write for clarity and effectiveness for your story, and don't revise your writing so it sounds and reads like the work of a famous author.)

Make your writing reflect you, and no one else.

1) Clichés

Clichés are words and phrases in the language that have been overused (raining cats and dogs, thunderous applause, bottled-up emotion, and so on). An author must strive for fresh, vibrant language. Whether clichés are present is a judgment that depends on one's experience in reading and one's perception of the originality of any word or phrase's vitality. Yet it is surprising how consistently experienced readers will judge clichés in specific works. Authors must be highly sensitive to the presence of any clichés in their writings and must remove them; clichés deaden the story and push readers away.

2) Word choice

Words must be accurate. ("He held her in his arms," *not* "He crushed her in his arms.").

Words must be appropriate to the context of the story and true to the narrative voice in action at the time of the word use. The following dialog does not fit for a character isolated in a black ghetto in New York City for life: "He had a bloody right to keep his mouth shut," Keshawn thought. Remove from your writing this type of mischosen word, and more subtle examples, so that you can be sure your words don't stretch meaning, are logical in the context of the character who is speaking, and do not detract from the story meaning or purpose.

Thesaurus use is both necessary and fun. Finding the right word should give every author a touch of satisfaction. If exploring alternatives for words in the story is a dreaded task, authors should reexamine their motivations for writing.

3) *Syntax*

Syntax. The order and relationship among the structural elements in sentences and phrases.

Using syntax that supports an author's prose is a skill acquired through practice. To develop syntactical excellence may require writing as many possibilities that can be thought of and then choosing the most effective one. Word positioning for best emphasis is one goal. Best placement of a modifier is another.

4) *Spelling and grammar*

Spelling and grammar are not just rules to irritate authors; they are agreed guidelines that, over centuries of continuous change, help clarify the prose for the reader. Correct spelling and grammar make the reading easier and more fluid for the reader, and clarify the meaning. Instances where stories use altered spelling or ungrammatical prose are often necessary, but they are created only as an alteration by an author who knows what is accepted as proper. As an author, don't believe out-of-control poor spelling and sloppy grammar is stylistic. It is just amateurish.

5) *Formatting*

Avoid fancy fonts that are now available on computers. Times or Times Roman are standard. For a manuscript submission, always leave ample (> 1.1) margins and double space the text. Keep the font size at 12 points; there are no exceptions.

M. Process of revision

Revision is a continuous process while creating a story, not an end step in story writing. Revision starts before the writing when the essential thinking about the story is active. Revision is important during the writing at all levels, from conflict and action, to the right word. Revision involves making changes in the story that will improve reader understanding and enjoyment, and it should be an inseparable part of an author's approach to storytelling.

Principles*-revision*

*Stories should be entertaining.
*Stories should enlighten or change existing thought.
*Writing fiction is creating a great story for the reader. Writing a memoir is telling with interest what has happened. To confuse your purpose decreases your effectiveness in each discipline. If memoir ideas restrict the telling of a literary story, restructure.
*Use the narrator to create drama. Ineffective narrator use is a common error in storytelling.
*Good storytelling depends on specific, not general, language; concrete, not abstract, ideas; fresh

voice; character consistency; avoidance of cuteness or self-importance.
*Stories should have a theme to create unity.
*Good modern stories avoid fatalism. Free will of characters is what drives a story.
*Stories are not essays on psychology. Psychological ideas in a story require dramatization. Don't analyze on the page.
*Back story (action or information that occurred before story beginning) is only effective as an integral part of a continuously progressing front story.
*Time is imbedded in characters, the prose, the reader. Time moves in a line. Failure to orient the reader to time causes confusion and the story telling fails.
*Stories must have the potential for movement. Conflict is established and then something must happen.
*Multiple drafts alone don't generate good stories. Each successive draft must change and improve the story, not just meet a writing schedule. Make revisions effective by addressing structure and what the reader needs to know.
*A metaphysical questions (abstract reasoning transcending physical matter and the laws of nature) are posed by characters, the narrator, or by the plot (dramatic structure). Metaphysical question answers everything the story poses, and nothing that occurs after the question is answered will change the story.

William H. Coles

Guidelines-*revision*

Essentials

1) When you read your work, are you engaged? Do you enjoy it? If you don't, even after hundreds of readings, your reader has little chance of enjoying it the first time through. Look for ways to better structure the story for tension and interest, more effective characterization, and increased drama.
2) Are the elements--diction, point of view, characterization, imagery, plot, and theme--completely addressed?
3) Check story for the most common reasons for story failure: one-character story, literal recall, too much internal reflection, back story, excessive exposition.
4) Was your outline effective? If not, identify errors and look for ways to strengthen unity, coherence, theme, characterization, and assure coherent time movement. When reviewing an outline, the drama should be inherently apparent and relate directly to the story.
5) Is the story told in dramatic scenes? Is drama ubiquitous, even in dialog, action, and narrative passages--and in every sentence?
6) Is theme clear? If not, restructure.
7) Is the essential conflict and resolution clear? Write all scenes with cause/effect in mind.

Quality of story telling

8) Are characters' and narrator's voices vibrant and interesting?
9) Are there spots in your writing where either tone, voice, plot, or dialogue is dampened and ineffective because of a mental image or idea carried from your own life experiences? If so, let your imagination revise.
10) Is there a consistent moral stance for the narrator and characters that is understood by the reader. Are you able to create tension in the story and movement in the plot by using differences in moral attitudes?
11) Are transitions elegant and dynamic? Are they relevant? Is the linking effective? Remember that line spaces are not transitions and should not replace a need for transition.
12) Are your inner story and outer story balanced? The most frequent error is too little outer story to contrast the inner story.
13) Is the story static because of failure to involve the narrator?
14) Check the story for clarity of differences in perspectives and diction (voice) between the narrator and characters. And remember, a narrator is always telling a story that has already happened, and that is often different than the characters experiencing the story in story-time.

Perfection

15) Are you sure there are enough possibilities for the characters to act? This is essential to maintain reader's belief in character and story.
16) Is the first-person point of view broad enough? Don't be afraid to expand the first-person character's view of the story—an "omniscient" first person. Although difficult to make seamless for the reader—so no rupture in smooth telling occurs—it provides maximum story detail.
17) When using multiple characters in a story, have you lost characters? Keep track of all characters—where they are, what they are thinking, what they're doing—even though most of the information will never be in the story.
18) Have you provided too much the reader didn't want to know (usually setting detail, recall, and reflection)? Have you provided too little of what readers wanted to know (characterization)?
19) Are your scenes longer in the middle than they are at the beginning and in the end? Keep a good balance and meet reader expectations.
20) Have you created the best voice for the narrator? Avoid sloppy or cute diction. And don't limit the narrator's intelligence.
21) Don't let the narrator comment on the characters too much. For example, "Jamie did not like ice cream. He didn't like Brussels sprouts either. In truth, he was relatively intolerant of all foods."

22) Don't let the narration go over the characters. Excessive telling about things may swamp required character action.
23) Don't let the narrator come too close to the character. The reader must have a sense of the narrator still telling the story and that the character has not taken over the storytelling. Characters are too busy being themselves and carrying the story action to provide the narrator ideas and details.
24) Have you withheld crucial story information from the reader to create tension? Revise. You should give the reader everything they need to know. Readers feel betrayed when information is withheld.
25) Have you stayed in a close point of view for too long so the story collapses? For example, "Tony saw the envelope on the desk, the crooked stamp, the scruffy corners. Pale blue too, the color Maggie always loved. And her handwriting! The cramped tails on the y's, the o's like pinholes, the r's flattened to almost straight lines. In a thousand years he could never mistake this writer." Revise and cut.

APPENDIX 1
WRITING IN THE MOMENT

In the moment writing is frequently referred to but rarely described, probably because many of in the moment skills are unique to the author and guidelines may not universally applicable. Still, authors must understand what in the moment is for them because in the moment provides immediacy and adds special tension to writing that may not be developed with other techniques.

In the moment writing is intense, and like anger, it is hard to sustain continuously for long periods. Excessive, particularly prolonged, use of in the moment writing may become counter productive and push the reader away.

Writing in the moment is achieved by word choice (avoiding abstractions, providing exact details, choosing accurate verbs), time management of scene, internal reflection with vitality, no passive constructions.

1. A descriptive scene

A man and his wife drove in a forty-five year old 1967 VW bus with their two children in the back seat. They argued over his recent affair with another woman. The bus sped along. Cars and trucks whizzed by on the opposite lane of a two-lane road. He refused to acknowledge his wife. Her anger mounted. She attacked him; he lost control so the van hit an oncoming car head on. They died.

2. Same scene as above written with in-scene action

Paul drove and Sarah had her arms wrapped around her knees in the passenger seat. It was a VW minibus from the sixties and the years had rusted the frame and two window in the back cracks and gapes were covered with surgical tape.

Paul looked straight-ahead. Sarah yelled, her face white with anger, not so much angry at his infidelity but at his self-righteousness about it all.

"Look at me!" she yelled, "Goddamn it! Look at me." She wanted to tell him it was over. One of the children cried in the back.

He remained expressionless. The VW picked up speed, straining at its limits. The sun glared near the horizon, it blinded him for an instant. He studied the central stripe on the two-lane road. A dump truck passed blowing a horn. He did not think he was over the centerline. A Volvo station wagon whizzed by.

As the sun began to set, Sarah screamed.
"You self-righteous bastard!"
A car headed toward them was small and red. A sedan.
"I will not let you humiliate me."
He held the speed, the glare made the centerline indistinct.

"Can't you say something," She pounded her fist in the air. "I've given you years. I deserve a few words."

"Go fuck yourself," he said softly.

She lunged toward him, using the power of her folded legs. With both hands she clutched the wheel, turning it from his grasp.

3. Same scene written in the moment

Sarah's scream stretched out and hurt his right ear. He would not talk to her. He consciously kept every muscle of his face an unrevealing mask, his eyes held to the road. He squinted in the glare of the sun. The engine whined, the loose body parts vibrated with an intermittent clamor. She came at him, he saw her from the side. She was sitting with her feet on the seat, her knees bent, and she just unwound toward him. He saw the red car a few hundred yards away. The sun blinded him again for a second and then was lost behind a line of trees. He clutched the wheel.

He tightened his grip but her quickness wrenched his hands from the wheel. The VW crossed the centerline; it was as if he could count each segment of the broken line now. He had his hands on the plastic of the wheel. He twisted to the right. Sarah was between his chest and the wheel. She was trying to turn. Her fists mechanically pounded his side.

The oncoming car was chili pepper red, the sun glinting off the surface, close enough that the closure zoomed large now. And then, the impact. Sarah's head cracked the window, an image etched in his mind, a star burst in the glass but no sound of her head splitting—but he thought he saw her brain, those enigmatic folds, and then her body ejection, shoulders first through the shards of glass. Her dress ripped exposing her leg, a piece of glass cutting to the bone so smooth and clean it was bloodless in the instant he saw it, and then she disappeared in a crush of folding metal and his world went dark.

Appendix 2
Scene Examples:
Variations of Narration, Point of View, Distance, Voice, Tense

1. Scene essence.

A man walks out of a hospital at night and joins a woman in a car. She starts the car and drives up ramp to expressway.

2. Scene: Third person point of view. Objective narration.

A young man in a white lab coat exited the hospital through the double automatic doors, looking left and right. He walked quickly to a red two-seater top-up convertible, with spoke-wheels gleaming in the bright lights of the hospital approach ramp, parked in a no-standing zone with front wheels on the pedestrian cross walk, headlights on, the engine running. The high beams flashed. He got in.

The car jerked forward, the whine of the manual shift higher with each gear change, as it climbed up the ramp to the connector heading North on I-75.[1]

---

[1] The last sentence confirms the position of the teller to be a few hundred feet away. Consistency of distance of point of view to action is at times desirable, but changing distance is often useful to present important details to the reader. Authors should be aware of distance in scenes.

3. Scene: Third person point of view. In-scene action. Objective.

Tom walked through the double automatic doors of the hospital, looking left and right. He walked to a red two-seater top-up convertible, with spoke-wheels gleaming in the bright lights, parked in a no-standing zone with front wheels on the pedestrian cross walk, headlights on, the engine running. The high beams flashed. He got in. His fiancée Jenny sat in the driver's seat.

"Hey, great wheels," he said. He closed the door, strapped in. He breathed in the scent of new-car leather. "You pick it up today?"

She didn't answer. She let out the clutch out and the car jerked forward. She shifted into third.

"You pleased?" he said.

She still did not speak. In three minutes, the car climbed up the ramp to the connector heading North on I-75.

"Ruptured globe," he explained. "My turn to help the residents."

She downshifted.

"Drunk got bashed with a pool cue. Lost an eye."

The car followed an eighteen-wheeler trailer truck.

"Asshole," she said taking her hand of the gearshift and showing her raised middle finger to the back of the truck. She flashed her lights. The truck moved over.

Tom kissed his fingertips and placed them on her lips for a few seconds. She didn't look at him. "Happy birthday," he said.

She passed a car and cut back in front, inches from the front bumper.

"Whoa," he said.

"Don't start."

He tightened his seat belt.

4. Scene: In-scene action. Two third-person points of view. Subjective.

Tom walked through the double automatic doors of the hospital, looking left and right for Jenny. Jenny sat in her new sports car with tinted windshields knowing he couldn't see her and refusing to signal him. He was five hours late for her birthday dinner with her parents.

He saw only one Jenny-looking car, a red two-seater top-up convertible, with spoke-wheels gleaming in the bright lights, parked in a no-standing zone with front wheels on the pedestrian cross walk, headlights on, the engine running. It was her birthday present and she had picked it up that afternoon. It had an ominous reptilian look in the night shadows. He got in.

"Hey, this is great," he said before closing the door, strapping in.

Jenny looked straight ahead but could still see his reflection in the windshield glass. He had the uncanny habit of looking fresh and eager at anytime of the day or night. Usually it pleased her, but tonight she was irritated.

She let the clutch out fast and the car jerked forward. She jammed it into third.

"You pleased?" he said. He meant the car. She had no idea that he wanted her happy. His comment was innocent. But she swore. They had that kind of relationship—often misunderstanding one another.[2]

They were on their way to dinner with her parents. With the sparse late-hour traffic, it would take about two hours. They would miss the family birthday dinner for her that was a tradition at the lake house.

Her mother was not particularly a good cook: she was expert in over baked turkey, cheese grits, broccoli mixed with canned mushrooms, and banana cream pie for desert.[3]

Within minutes, the car sped up the ramp onto the connector to head North on I-75.

"Ruptured globe," he said. It was his way to apologize. "My turn to help the residents."

She downshifted and the engine whined.

"Drunk got bashed with a pool cue," he added, "Lost an eye."

She tailgated an eighteen-wheeler trailer truck that was slowing travel in a passing lane.

"Asshole," she said. She flashed her lights until the truck moved over.

Tom kissed his fingertips and placed them on her lips for a few seconds. The gesture surprised him as

---

[2] This could be from a narrator or one of the characters.
[3] This statement acts as a narrator comment, although either Tom or Jenny could be attributed without change in meaning.

silly and awkward. But he wanted to reach out to her. She had every right to be angry.

She didn't look at him. "Happy birthday," he said.

She accelerated the car past a pickup truck and cut back into the lane inches from the pickup's front bumper.

"Whoa," Tom said.

"Don't start."

He held back a response. Jenny's driving had never been good. It was the way she lived her life, always in danger.

He tightened his seat belt.

5. Scene: First person (Tom), no narrator voice.

I walked through the double automatic doors of the hospital, looking left and right for Jenny. She would be in her new car--her birthday present. There was only one Jenny-looking car, a red two-seater top-up convertible, with spoke-wheels gleaming in the bright lights, parked in a no-standing zone with front wheels on the pedestrian cross walk, headlights on, the engine running. The high beams flashed impatiently. I doubled over to look in the low passenger side window to be sure it was her. In the dim interior I could see her profile. She didn't turn her head to me.

"Hey, this is great," I said.

Jenny wasn't talking. She let the clutch out fast and the car jerked forward. She jammed it into third.

"You pleased?" I said. She must have picked it up at the dealership this morning. Saturday.

We were on our way to her birthday dinner with her parents. A two-hour drive to the family lake house. I was five hours late and too late to go by my place to pick up clothes and toiletries for the night. In minutes, Jenny revved up on the ramp to the connector to head North on I-75.

"Ruptured globe," I said. "My turn to help the residents."

She downshifted, her clutch movements already smoother at the higher speeds, and the engine whined.

"Drunk got bashed with a pool cue. Lost an eye."

She tailgated an eighteen-wheeler trailer truck that was slowing travel in a passing lane.

"Asshole," she said. I thought she meant me but she flashed her lights until the truck moved over.

I kissed my fingertips and placed them on her lips for a few seconds. She didn't look at me. "Happy birthday," I said.

She passed a car and cut back in front, inches from the front bumper.

"Whoa," I said.

"Don't start."

She was a shitty driver even before she got a sports car, indifferent to the basics of a safe journey like driving within the speed limits and following cars at a reasonable distance. She was combative; other drivers were enemies to her will rather than comrades with travel needs. I tightened my seat belt.

6. Scene: First person with narrator components.

Grady Hospital was at the intersections of three major interstates, a perfect position to receive injuries from every part of the Southeast. On call doctors rarely slept and stayed on past their shifts to complete treatment on their patients.[4]

I was late and she was angry.[5] It wasn't reasonable but it was understandable. I walked through the double automatic doors of the hospital, looking left and right for Jenny. She had picked up her new car this morning--her birthday present.[6] There was only one Jenny-looking car, a red two-seater top-up convertible, with spoke-wheels gleaming in the bright lights, parked in a no-standing zone with front wheels on the pedestrian cross walk, headlights on, the engine running. The color red boosted her confidence and suited her well. The high beams flashed impatiently. I walked down the ambulance ramp.

---

[4] First person with narrator components allow scene view from some distance and providing information that might be out of the range of the senses and the experiences of the first person character. The narrator presence has been exaggerated for the example.

[5] A narrator's statement, that is outside the reasonable knowledge of the first person--he hasn't seen her yet--but acceptable (and often useful) to the reader.

[6] With narrator information already provided, this statement is not questioned. If a narrator presence is not established, the careful reader might pause and wonder if this statement is unreliable since it is possible the first person might not know it.

She tapped the horn to get my attention.[7] I doubled over to look in the low passenger side window to be sure it was her. In the dim interior I saw her profile. She wouldn't turn her head to me.[8] She was that angry.

"Hey, this is great," I said.

Jenny wasn't talking. She let the clutch out fast and the car jerked forward. She jammed it into third, skipping over second by inexperience rather than for efficiency.

"You pleased?" I said.

It was Saturday. Raining in New York, windy in Oregon, but here in Atlanta it was a sweltering ninety-eight degrees.

At the lake house her parents had already eaten. Food had been wrapped and refrigerated waiting for us to arrive. It was no great loss for me. Her mother always fried chicken, baked potatoes, overcooked vegetables, and made banana cream pie with chunks of banana too big to swallow.

Jenny's law school training made her suspect doctors of inherently misleading.

"Ruptured globe," I said. "My turn to help the residents."

She was suspicious. She couldn't trust me even after six months of engagement.

---

[7] This is a narrator function. Some teachers of creative writing would demand restructuring to clarify the first person could reasonably give this information. For example, "A horn blew, I thought it was from Jenny—trying to get my attention.

[8] Narrator function. First person character expresses intent of another character. If the story telling contract between narrator and reader is established, this narrator function is acceptable and effective.

She downshifted, her clutch movements already smoother at the higher speeds, and the engine whined.

"Drunk got bashed with a pool cue. Lost an eye."

She tailgated an eighteen-wheeler trailer truck that was slowing travel in a passing lane.

"Asshole," she said. I thought she meant me but she flashed her lights until the truck moved over.

I kissed my fingertips and placed them on her lips for a few seconds. She didn't look at me. "Happy birthday," I said.

She passed a car and cut back in front, inches from the front bumper. She never saw the bumper, it never occurred to her to worry.

"Whoa," I said.

"Don't start." She was tired of my habitual backseat driving, new car or no new car. But in truth, she was a shitty driver even before she got a sports car, indifferent to the basics of a safe journey like driving within the speed limits and following cars at a reasonable distance. She was combative; other drivers were enemies to her will rather than comrades with travel needs. I tightened my seat belt.[9]

---

[9] Still another example of using first person with narrator functions where very valuable information can be succinctly presented to the reader and enhance the story. If established early in the story, this technique is readily accepted by the reader, and improves effectiveness of narrator delivering story through the inherent limitations of a first person. The technique also lessons the danger of awkward constructions such as "I instinctively knew Jenny would not like..." or "I would later discover Jenny's parents had already consumed their part of the birthday dinner . . ."

7. Two scenes. Verb Tense Comparison; past and present.

A. Past

Tom walked through the double automatic doors of the hospital, looking left and right for Jenny. Jenny sat in her new sports car with tinted windshields knowing he couldn't see her and refusing to signal him. He was five hours late for her birthday dinner with her parents.

He saw only one Jenny-looking car, a red two-seater top-up convertible, with spoke-wheels gleaming in the bright lights, parked in a no-standing zone with front wheels on the pedestrian cross walk, headlights on, the engine running. It had an ominous reptilian look in the night shadows. He got in.

"Hey, this is great," he said before closing the door, strapping in.

Jenny looked straight ahead but could still see his reflection in the windshield glass. He had the uncanny habit of looking fresh and eager at anytime of the day or night. Usually it pleased her, but tonight she was irritated.

She let the clutch out fast and the car jerked forward. She jammed it into third.

B. Present

Tom walks through the double automatic doors of the hospital, looking left and right for Jenny. Jenny sits in her new sports car with tinted windshields knowing he can't see her and refusing to signal him. He is five hours late for her birthday dinner with her parents.

He sees only one Jenny-looking car, a red two-seater top-up convertible, with spoke-wheels gleaming in the bright lights, parked in a no-standing zone with front wheels on the pedestrian cross walk, headlights on, the engine running. It has an ominous reptilian look in the night shadows. He gets in.

"Hey, this is great," he says before closing the door, strapping in.

Jenny looks straight ahead but can still see his reflection in the windshield glass. He has the uncanny habit of looking fresh and eager at anytime of the day or night. Usually it pleases her, but tonight she is irritated.

She lets the clutch out fast and the car jerks forward. She jams it into third.[10]

---

[10] Authors often use present tense in stories to generate a sense of immediacy but often the sense of immediacy quickly dissipates and the awkward constructions caused by present tense become irritating. For example, "He has the uncanny habit of looking fresh and eager at anytime of the day or night." This is an observation of things he has done in the past. To express in the present tense borders on speculation and causes time confusion. The character could say "He had the uncanny habit . . ." but then the switching from present to past tense and back again becomes awkward. These problems of time clarity with present tense decrease the usefulness of the tense in a fiction story; the use of present tense may also leave a sense of artificiality to the story as compared to the solidity of the past tense as a purveyor of reasonable and accurate story details.

8. In scene action. Limited third person point of view.

Comment. *Note the close (sometimes thought of as tight) viewpoint on scene action. This refers to proximity of viewpoint to action. Also, there is use of character internal reflection (thoughts and feelings). There is a tendency to overuse the thoughts of characters at expense of action in scene, and this occurs here but is not revised to enhance the example.*

Tom had an emergency case, a serious eye injury, and he was five hours late when he phoned Jenny to pick him up at the hospital. He walked through the double automatic doors of the hospital, looking left and right for Jenny's new car—a red two-seater top-up convertible, a birthday present from her parents that she had picked up that afternoon. He saw it parked in a no-standing zone with front wheels on the pedestrian cross walk, headlights on, the engine running. The high beams flashed; Jenny was pissed. He doubled over to look in the low passenger side window to be sure it was she. He got in.

"Hey, this is great," he said before closing the door, strapping in.

Jenny wasn't talking.

She let the clutch out fast and the car jerked forward. She jammed it into third.

"You like it?" he asked.

They were on their way to dinner with Jenny's parents, a two-hour drive to the family lake house. It was a family tradition to have birthdays at the lake. Jenny's mother, with no variation, had a baked turkey, cheese grits, broccoli mixed with canned mushrooms, and banana cream pie for desert. She was a predictable cook, brought up in a Southern family privileged to have a full time servant who prepared meals, and not worthy of anticipation.

Tom looked at the dash clock--five minutes to nine. If he had been on time, he would have insisted they go by his place to pick up clothes and toiletries for the night. But Jenny was angry as hell, and he decided not to ask. He would have to borrow toothpaste and brush his teeth with his finger. When the car neared the ramp to the connector to head North on I-75, Jenny revved up the motor.

"Ruptured globe," he said. It was his attempt at reconciliation. "My turn to help the residents."

But Jenny had been waiting for five hours with little to do. She wasn't going to give in by letting him think she wasn't displeased. She downshifted unnecessarily and the engine whined.

"Drunk got bashed with a pool cue. Lost an eye," Tom tried again.

She believed he loved surgery more than going to the lake and that there were others who could have taken the case. Her driving irritated him—he was a cautious driver--as she tailgated an eighteen-wheeler trailer-truck that was slowing travel in a passing lane.

"Asshole," she said. She flashed her lights until the truck moved over.

Tom felt bad about making her so distressed. Family was important to her. Birthdays too. He kissed his fingertips and placed them on her lips for a few seconds. She still refused to look at him.

"Happy birthday," he said.

She passed a car and cut back in front, inches from the front bumper.

"Whoa," he said.

"Don't start."

For the first time since their engagement, now more than six months, he saw her reckless driving as a tool she used against him. It was a matter of safety for him: drive within the speed limits and follow cars at a reasonable distance. He tightened his seat belt resigned to making it all work.

9. Scene as transition.

Comment. The use of a specific scene draft will depend on the effect on the story. It is probable an author would find most of the above drafts of this scene: 1) lacking drama needed, 2) providing strained characterization, 3) taking too much time in relation to plot contribution and/or amount of character development, 4) showing the inner conflicts (and his feigned disregard) do not mesh well with outer conflicts (lateness, driving ability, personality differences.) Most commonly, any one of scenes 1-9 would be discarded. But still reader orientation may be necessary. A transition can be used.

Jenny picked up Tom at the hospital and they drove to her parents' place on Lake Lanier.[11]

---

[11] This is short, but with the single purpose to move the characters, it is effective. Doesn't the quality and length of the prose and lack of exposition seem a better choice for the scene action and contribution to story? New writers are tempted to do more with this type of transition. "Susan, in her business suit, picked Tom up—he was still in his lab coat—and drove him to her father's two story five bedroom house on the shore of Lake Lanier in the heart of the newest and socially most prominent development." This strives for too much.

APPENDIX 3
SAMPLE OUTLINES

This partial outline of the first part of a story describes scenes in order with setting, time, and the emotional arc of a protagonist.

Scene	Time	Jean-Luc
1. Paris House	1793	Desire. Honor his parents. Be good Christian.
2. House	Day 1	Optimism about mother having her miracle. Need—to sell lamps for money to help his mother. Has desire to help.
3. House	Day 6	Grieves over father. Needs to meet his father's challenge to save his mother.
4. Place de la Concorde	Day 7 AM	Humiliated by cruel humor of aristocratic girl. Perceived failure with women.
5. House	Day 7 PM	Need to please, helps father get mother to good health. Fear of her death. Tries to save father. Does not know but believes he caused father's death.
6. Place de Greve	Day 8 AM	Instinctively tries to save victim. Fear of death—sense of justice. Guilt at failure.
7. On North Road	Day 10 AM	Etc.

It is often useful to outline functions separately, although scene number (to orient time) should always be indicated. Here are emotional arcs (partial) of additional characters with scenes identified.

Charlotte	Auguste
1. Resentment over injustice of impending death. Unforgiving. Ornery.	1. Desires image of his wife in past--playful, young, loving.
2. Unkind. Refuses to feel when husband dies.	2. Need to provide even when dying.
3. Increasing need for miracle. Aware of her son, but fails to see his need for praise.	3. Death.
4.	4.
5. Grief that miracle is thwarted again. Cannot face loss of husband. Grief is anger against Jean-Luc.	5.
6. Anxiety over shrinking time. No love for failure of men in her life.	6.
7. Etc.	7.

INDEX

Action, 13
Action, 65-66
Action, and recall and reflection, 65,
Action, defined 9
Arc, story, 65
Attitude, story unity, 7
Attitudes, author's, 4
Attitudes, fine-tuning, 4-7
Attribution, modifiers, 35
Author, creating story, 43
Author, differences from narrator, 43-47
Author, morality, 41
Author, settings and, 18
Author, time, 16
Authorial intrusion, 34
Awakenings, and endings, 28
Back story, 71
Beginning, defined, 26
Beginning, principles, 27
Bronte, Charlotte, *Jane Eyre*, 48-49
Change and discovery, 9-10
Character, "I", 45-49
  answer to questions, 35
  conflict, 24
  desires, 31
  distance, 59
  from life, 25
  integrated with plot, 23
  lost, 25
  motivation, 25
  time, 15
  unified overview, 25
  voice, 60-61
Characterization, guidelines, 24-25
Characterization, principles,
Characterization, principles, 23-24
Characters, coming alive, 20-21
Characters, development, 24
Characterization, 19
Clichés, defined, 68
Communication, story and, 37
Conflict, 13
  action and, 13
  character, 24
  defined, 9
  in drama. 30
  in-scene, 13
  major, 12
  telling and, 13
  types, 13, 30
Conflict/action/resolution, 13
Conflicts, verbal, 13
Contents, Table of, 1
Continuous fictional dream, 58
Core Questions, 5-7

Creativity, in structure, 10
Dialogue, guidelines, 35
Description, narrative, 19
Description, narrative, example, 66
Desires, show not tell, 24
Desires, character, 31
Desires, need to be powerful, 24
Dialogue, 32-35
   consistent voice and, 34
   example of improved, 33
   fiction, 32
   guidelines, 35
   inappropriate responses in, 25
   principles, 34
   purposes, 32
   rhythm, 33, 35
Dialogue, example of failed, 33
Distance, 59
   character, 59
   how created, 59
   point of view, 52
   relation to action, 59
   shifting, example of, 59-60
   narrator, 59
Drama, 6
   in conflict, 30
   in narration, 64
   principles, 65

Dream, continuous fictional, 58
Elements, outline, 12
Emotion, and feelings, 22
Emotions, and story moment, 25
End, defined, 28
Ending, ineffective, 29
Ending, principles, 28-29
Ending, reversals, 28
Endings, something new, 28
Engage reader, in-scene, 65
Engage the reader, 58
Enlightenment, story, 70
Entertaining, story, 70
Entertainment, story life and, 38
Fame, 5-6
Feelings, 22-23
Feelings, and sentimentality, 22
Feelings, telling, 22
Filter, narrator, 48
First person
   close, 56
   limitation, 46
   principles, 55-56
   reliability, 45-46
   self-knowledge,
   use,
First sentence, 27
Flashbacks, 17
Formatting, 69-70
Genre fiction, 26

Goals, 10
Grammar, 69
Guideline, setting, 19
Guidelines
    characterization, 24-25
    dialogue, 35
    middle, 27-28
    outline, 12
    point of view, 57
    revision, 72-73
    space for the reader, 62
    theme and meaning, 42-43
    transitions, 30
Hero, defined, 40
"I" character, as narrator, 49
Imagination, reader, 61
Imagination, 5
In scene action, example, 92-93
In the moment, 17-18, 77-80
In the moment, writing 77-80
Information, withheld, 75
Inner story, balanced, 73
In-scene narrator, example, 47-48
In-scene showing, example, 14
In-scene, reader engagement and, 65
In-scene, conflicts 14
In-scene, example, 66
In-scene, showing, 13
Intelligence, narrator, 74
Internal reflection, 21
Intrusion, authorial, 34
Jane Eyre, Charlotte Bronte, 48-49
Language, 67
    clarity, 67
    grammar, 67
    punctuation, 67
    self-criticism, 67
    vocabulary, 67
Literary story, 3
Logic, time, 16
Manuscript, 69-70
Meaning, defined, 40
Memoir, 49
Memoir, and fiction writing, 70
Metaphysical questions, defined, 71
Middle, defined, 27
Middle, guidelines, 27-28
Modifiers in attribution, 35
Morality, author's, 41
Morality, defined, 40
Motivations, character, 31
Movement, story, revision, 71
Narration, drama, 64
Narration, principles 49
Narrative bridge, 16
Narrative description, and in scene, 66

Narrative description, settings and, 19
Narrative telling, example, 14
Narrative telling, conflicts, 13
Narrator
   and closeness to character, 75
   differences from author, 43-47
   distance, 59
   intelligence and, 74
   morality and author, 41
   reliability, 45-46
   reliability, 52
   story failure and,
   telling story, 43
   time, 15
   too close, 75
Narrative description, example, 66
Omniscient point of view, 53
Opinion, Propaganda and, 6
Options, character, 21-22
Outer story, balanced, 73
Outline, 11-12
   examples, 97-98
   guidelines, 12
   principles, 12
Paradox, defined, 40
Plot, 26-32
Plot, action, 31
Plot, emotional, 31
Plot, inner, 31
Plot, outer, 32
Point of view, 50-57
   camera analogy, 50
   close too long, 75
   defined, 50
   definitions, 50
   distance, 52
   first person, 48
   guidelines, 57
   manner of considering, 50
   omniscient, 53
   position in space, 50
   principles, 53
   reasoned mental attitude, 50
   reflexive, 57
   related issues, 51
   restrictive rules, 51
Political purpose, 42-43
Presence, narrator's, 34
Principle, voice, 61
Principles
   beginning, 27
   characterization, 23-24
   dialogue, 34
   drama, 65
   ending, 28-29
   first person, 55-56
   outline, 12
   point of view, 53
   revision, 70-71
   setting, 18
   space for the reader, 62

Prose, elevated, 10-11
Prose, fancy, 6
Prose, not endpoint, 11
Prose, over-extended, 66
Prose, over-extended, example, 66
Questions, character's, 35
Questions, core, 5-7
Questions, metaphysical, defined, 71
Reader engagement, missteps, 58
Reader involvement, story life, 38-39
Reader surprise, how achieved, 20
Reader, imagination, 61
Reader, led not forced, 20
Reader, space, 61
Reader, time, 16
Reader's wants, 37
Reflection, internal, 21
Reflexive point of view, 57
Reliability and
    first person, 45-46
    narrator, 46, 52
    point of view, 51-52
Resolution, 13
Resolution, clarity, revision,
Resolution, defined, 9
Resolutions, clarity, 28
Response, character, example, 21-22
Responses, inappropriate, 25
Reversal, story life and, 38
Reversals, and endings, 28
Revision
    essentials, 72
    guidelines, 72-73
    principles, 69
    process of, 70-75
    time, 71
Scene
    as transition example, 94-95
    conflict, 13
    descriptive, 77-78
    examples, 81-95
    first person examples, 85-89
    in the moment, 79-80
    in-scene action, 78-7
    length, 74
    resolution, 13
    single character, 13
    third person examples, 81-85
Scenes, 12
Scenes, one-character, 24
Sentiment, implied, example, 64
Sentence, first, 27
Sentimentality, 63-64
    defined, 63
    examples, 64
    genre fiction and, 63
    subjective, 63
Setting, 18-19
Setting, guideline, 19

Setting, plot and character, 18
Setting, principles, 18
Setting, travel-folder, 18
Single character scene, 13
Space for reader, guidelines, 62
Space for the reader, principles, 62
Space, for reader, 61
Spelling, 69
Start, of story, 27
Stereotypes, 20-21
Stereotypes, poor characterization and, 20
Story life
    action, 39
    defined, 37-38
    entertainment, 38
    reader involvement, 38-39
    value, 39-40
Story
    and psychological ideas, 71
    arc, 65
    as jigsaw puzzle, 7
    history, 3
    learning and life, 37
    literary, 3
    time, 15
    time, author and narrator, 47
Storyteller, great, 4
Structure, and story, 9-11

Surprise, 20
Syntax, defined, 69
Table of Contents, 1
Tense and time, 17
Tense, past and present compared, 90-91
Theme and meaning, guidelines, 42-43
Theme, defined, 40
Time condensation, 16
Time
    tense and, 17
    author and, 16
    character and, 15
    establishing, 14
    in revision, 71
    logic and, 16
    narrator and, 15
    reader and, 16
    story and, 15
    story, author and narrator and, 47
Transitions, 29-30, 73
Transition, as scene, 94-95
Transitions, guidelines, 30
Unit, a story as, 7
Voice
    character's, 60-61
    defined, 60
    narrator, 74
    principle, 61
Withheld information, 75
Word choice, 68

Acknowledgement

Over the last nine years, I have sought the best teachers and writers to shape my understanding of writing a fictional story. Although each has contributed to my concept of literary story in unique and varied ways, none has made a direct contribution to the manuscript or is responsible for the content. I have taken workshops with Peter Ho Davies, Clark Blaise, Nancy Zafris, Elizabeth McCracken, Susan Straight, Christopher Tilghman, Karl Iagnemma, Bret Lott, Bharati Mukherjee, Tom Barbash, Kellie Wells, Lynn Freed, Richard Bausch, Jill McCorkle, John Casey, Margo Livesey, Tony Early, Michael Ray, Tamara Straus, Carol Edgarian, Jonathan Lethem, Sharyn McCrumb, Michael Parker, Abigail DeWitt, Rosemary Danielle, Lisa Borders, Gordon Mennenga; studied in semester academic courses with John Biguenet, Noel Polk, David Bottoms, Lisa Borders; worked with mentors Tom Jenks, Dianne Benedict, Anne Wood, Ben George, and Otonne Ricci; and attended conferences with Michael Cunningham, Jane Smiley, Robert Olen Butler, Joyce Carol Oates, Jack Driscoll, Dennis LeHane, and others.

WHC

Printed in the United States
79132LV00007B/13-15